ONE WAY
AF584397

SANDY WEIR

Other People's Homes

SUBURBAN KERB APPEAL

First published by Affirm Press in 2023
Boon Wurrung Country
28 Thistlethwaite Street
South Melbourne VIC 3205
affirmpress.com.au

10 9 8 7 6 5 4 3 2

A catalogue record for this book is available from the National Library of Australia

ISBN: 9781922992048 (hardback)

Cover design by Luke Causby, Blue Cork © Affirm Press
Internal design by Emily Thiang © Affirm Press
Typeset in Plantin by Monotype
Printed and bound in China by C&C Offset Printing Co. Ltd.

To all the lovely folks who live in the homes that stop me in my tracks: thanks for not shooing me away. Thanks for coming outside for a chat, giving me gardening tips, giving me life advice and telling me all about your places.

You are all heritage-worthy in my opinion.

‘Fascinating and delightful. If I was a house, I’d want to be in this book.’

Cal Wilson

‘*Other People’s Homes* is a magnificent celebration of Australian suburbia. It captures the eclectic array of architecture and design from all corners of the country, reflecting the essence of our rich diversity and history. Sandy is to be congratulated on documenting this precious treasure-trove.’

Georgie Gardner

‘A sublime celebration of the weird and wonderful places we call home.’

Jacinta Parsons

‘I always find it amazing how the front of houses can look on film. Sandy’s eye shows a unique insight into Australian homes.’

Gracie Otto

'*Other People's Homes* allows us to be what we all are at heart: nosy. Its purposeful curation of Australian abodes lets us have a stickybeak and celebrate the eclectic nature of this country's suburban infrastructure, while appreciating the difference between a house and a home.'

Maria Lewis

'*Other People's Homes* is my favourite comforting reminder that despite mass efforts to be homogeneous, a person can't help but try to build a castle in the middle of a suburban block.'

Natalie Tran

'What started as one of my favourite Instagram accounts is now one of my favourite books. An immersion in the beauty and awe that is suburban Australia from a time gone by.'

Samantha Wills

'There's no place like other people's homes.'

Samuel Johnson OAM

My dad used to say it's important to have a hobby that keeps you off the street. I spend my spare time wandering, admiring and having a bit of a stickybeak. But in the best, most polite way possible. Australian suburbia is an underestimated source of treasure. That is not a reference to real-estate prices; it's a nod to heartfelt value.

I take pictures of houses that remind us of where we grew up or where we wish we had grown up, where we were happy or where we thought we would be happy. Houses we walked past on the way to school, to meet friends in the park, for a sneaky kiss in a lane, on the way to our first jobs and on the way home. They represent where we came from and where we are going. Or where we want to go. All of the homes were once brand new and shiny – much-loved symbols of hard work and achievement. Many of them may well end up demolished one day, as fads and fashion move on. They might end up painted grey or hidden by a carport, but what's captured here in this book is a snapshot of a disappearing Australia.

I wander around, I look, I take pictures. I don't focus on any particular kind of architecture, but I have my favourites, though none are defined by a particular style, because I love everything from the humble fibro to the brick with concrete lion show-off joints. Along the way I've met architecture obsessives, MCM purists, retro lovers, Art Deco devotees, crazy paving nuts, migrant architecture aficionados, beach shackers, brick admirers, urbex chasers, wrought-iron addicts, fibro followers, Tudor tragics, symmetry buffs, wacky-house enthusiasts, militant Modernists, stone junkies, chimney disciples, terrace zealots, A-frame fans, pareidolia preferers and flats fanatics. I love chatting to them all.

And when I am strolling and stopping to admire, quite often the owners pop out like a champagne cork to ask what I'm doing, then end up telling me all about their house, their lives, their husbands, their families. It's wonderful.

Other times, after posting the pics to my Instagram, conversations ensue and I develop personal connections with people whose homes I have captured, or someone will tell me they know someone who lived there or used to live there, or I hear about the parties that were held in the house. One day, I was advised I'd been to parties in one of the Bondi Art Deco blocks I was coveting.

Sometimes, after seeing my photo of their house, people invite me over for tea or cocktails, for freshly made baklava or to take home some chokos. I'm told the histories of the houses and sent old photos. I've talked to the bricklayers or their relatives, the daughter of a pebble-creter and proud grandson of a wrought-iron master. When I started looking for houses by Italian architect Gino Volpato, I was delighted to meet members of his family and also the people who live in the houses he designed.

People tell me all the time of places I should go, and where to find a house they know I'd like. I spend a lot of time walking. I initially started wandering because my dog died, and I couldn't bear being in the house alone. I was missing my dog and feeling lonely. *Other People's Homes* has led me to find a lovely community of like-minded people. People who have respect for the houses in our suburbs and what they mean. Many of the houses I snap will never have heritage protection, many won't be there the next time I walk past, but they remind me to cherish what we have now and help me remember what is already gone. Being present, paying attention and marvelling at the wondrous differences that humans bring to the spaces they live in. I don't think my dad would mind me wandering the streets to do that.

Other People's Homes is an accidentally curated collection that celebrates the quirky, the innovative, the show stoppers, the elegantly decaying and the absolutely delightful homes hiding in plain view. I hope this collection hits you right in the nostalgia gland and gives you a smile.

And if you see me walking down your street or taking a photo of your house, please come and say hi … I promise I won't park out the front.

Sandy Weir's Instagram account *Other People's Homes* is not about the architecture of Australian homes, or the lack of it.

She sees the loss, the love, the hope, the ambition they represented, and the humour.

Unlike other accounts that are critical of architectural car crashes, Weir has no time for the naysayers.

In an interview with *The Sydney Morning Herald*, she told me how she swerved when she spotted a home designed by Italian Australian architect Gino Volpato. He didn't win awards, but hearts.

His work was as much loved by the families that treasured his homes as those who lived in houses designed by a more famous immigrant architect, Harry Seidler.

Weir's posts have heightened my awareness of the variety of homes, how they reflect our personalities and desires. Sometimes, a balcony shaped like a toothy grin makes me laugh. When it does, I thank Sandy Weir for seeing something that we all missed.

Julie Power – Senior Reporter,
Sydney Morning Herald

Welcome

001 *Reservoir, Victoria*

Welcome to the urban jungle.

***002** Concord, New South Wales*

'The curve is more powerful than the sword.' – Mae West

003 Richmond, Victoria

Every time you are tempted to order the smashed avo, think about how you could own this house instead.

004 Albury, New South Wales

All those times I just rocketed past Albury, who knew what treasures lay beyond the highway?

Saad Milham Abikhair was the owner-builder of this beauty, completed in 1950.

His family established Albury's most famous department store.

Just look at those features:

- ✓ waterfall facade
- ✓ beautiful staircase
- ✓ deep eyebrows
- ✓ commanding attitude
- ✓ steel-framed windows
- ✓ fab mint-green highlights.

005 Fitzroy, Victoria

You must see The Cairo Flats, they said. This Modernist block of apartments was built in 1936 and is designed by architect Acheson Best Overend.

I was sitting defeated at the locked gates of the building when a nice man said, 'Would you like to see inside?'

What an afternoon. Two long-term owners gave me a tour and I took eleventy-hundred pics. This one shows the famous concrete cantilever staircase, thought to be the first of its kind in the world.

006 Maroubra, New South Wales

I get a *What Ever Happened to Baby Jane?* vibe here.

007 Kew, Victoria

That car is the cherry on the top. *Phoar.*

You gotta love folks who match their car to their house. If that's what they consigned to the carport, imagine what they might have inside the garage?

For the record, the car's a Sunbeam – either Alpine or Tiger – and also for the record, I don't care how phoar is spelled, but thanks.

008 *Sans Souci, New South Wales*

Like an ice cream waiting to melt.

009 Toorak, Victoria

I was actually looking for the Swedish church nearby when a patch of colour burst through the hedge. *Boom.* Caringal Flats were designed in 1948 by architect John William Rivett, and the building was constructed in 1951. The colourful flat-roofed apartment block is of architectural significance to the State of Victoria. It's very tall. And the whole vibe is very flamingo.

010 *Chatswood, New South Wales*

Hilton, a Romanesque Revival house, was heritage listed in 1999 in response to an attempt to add a Cape Cod extension. It was designed by Albert Borchard and built in 1903. Apparently, it's haunted. I find the Chatswood Westfield scarier.

011 *Northcote, Victoria*

Number 275 has style and texture to spare.

012 *Elizabeth Bay,*
New South Wales

My friend and I have been discussing how superb it would be to have a drink on one of these balconies. Built in 1939, the Chatsbury building has *the* craziest steep driveway, a partially castellated roofline and those martini-perfect balconies. Chatsbury is an Elizabeth Bay icon; it's just soooooo stylish.

013 *Reservoir, Victoria*

You know you love it. From the gift that is Rezza.

014 Randwick, New South Wales

A patchwork masterpiece.

016 *Maroubra, New South Wales*

Persistence pays. I went back a few times hoping the cars wouldn't be in the driveway. On the third visit: bingo.

This house was my introduction to, and the beginning of my obsession with, the brilliance of Gino Volpato. A Modernist architect and designer, Gino Volpato's work is polarising in its unique boldness, and has seen a surge in popularity since his death in 2005. I believe he may be responsible for more U-turns than any other architect in Sydney's history. In a sea of grey-on-grey boxes, he dazzles.

015 *Elwood, Victoria*

Built in the 1950s, this waterfall-style house has the most fabulous turquoise trim. I'm no Miss Marple, but a bit of amateur sleuthing leads me to conclude that this place is the result of a subdivision of a grand Victorian-era property. I didn't even notice the neighbouring 1891 beauty because turquoise trim.

017 Coburg North, Victoria

Oh, hello. That room on the right-hand side where you can see straight through to the fab fern? Swoon.

018 *Canberra, Australian Capital Territory*

A temporary shelter from the weather for Ken Behrens and his family on the way out to Tuggeranong for a feed. It's Canberra AF.

019 *Gosford, New South Wales*

Is that your real hair? Fancy coming back to mine for a bit of Rapunzel-ing and a pizza?

020 *Bendigo, Victoria*

Beach shacks of Bendigo.

021 *Maribyrnong, Victoria*

Peacocks represent royalty in some cultures. These gates are certainly majestic, and as rare as royalty in the burbs.

022 Brookvale, New South Wales

Brookvale: home to the Sea Eagles, The Mall, Col Crawford and Milroy, a heritage-listed Art Deco Spanish Mission extravaganza with a bit of ocean-liner style chucked in. The delightful fan motif is continued inside, so I'm told. It was on *Selling Houses Australia* a while back, but didn't sell.

023 Shepparton, Victoria

Suddenly speechless in Shepparton.

024 Arncliffe, New South Wales

This place looks like someone nice lives there.

025 Fitzroy North, Victoria

Piano keys.

027 *Geelong, Victoria*

If I had a pool room this house would go *straight* there. The owner has been living here since his dad built it.

026 *Banksia, New South Wales*

Why travel to Rome when you can chuck a coin in here?

028 *Wangaratta, Victoria*

When driving to Melbourne from the northern states, stop in Wangaratta, where they have the best sandwiches (at the petrol station) and the best fence *in the world!*

029 *Bondi, New South Wales*

Goes to Bondi:

- ❍ Takes pic of colourful Art Deco apartments.
- ❍ Has an expensive juice that will make them a better person.
- ❍ Spends time considering how fab it would be to live so close to a beach again.

030 *Letterboxes*

At some point someone decided that letterboxes disguised as wood was a cracker idea.

031 *Eaglemont, Victoria*

Round breezeblocks. Round. This building is an absolute ripper. These sixteen company title flats known as Greenmount Court were designed in 1960 and built in '61. As the ad said: 'Spacious Living at a Sensible Price'.

It's the fashion-forward work of Polish architect John Holgar (1922–2006), who was a member of the Polish resistance during the war, and Helen Holgar (1923–2012). Initially sidelined by the mainstream profession, the pair's output developed a loyal fan base and has recently been re-evaluated by critics. I learned all this, and more, from a terrific notice on the ground floor.

032 Goulburn, New South Wales

Just like Goulburn, this is so many things.

- Those tiled steps are divine.
- This door is a Traffic-Stopper.
- Especially because it's red.
- And a circle.
- That brick circle above the door.

033 Castlecrag, New South Wales

Meet Panglos: Google says the name 'comes from Greek *pan* meaning "all", and *glossa* meaning "tongue", suggesting glibness and talkativeness'.

It's by Walter Burley Griffin and Eric Nicholls, built in 1939.

That cool castle bit is a Martello tower. Apparently, there are only two in the southern hemisphere – the other one, school excursion fave Fort Denison, is in Sydney Harbour.

034 Seddon, Victoria

There's a jaunty confidence to this place I find very appealing.

036 *Canberra, Australian Capital Territory*

Canberra being quite a fenceless place, front yards are very important.

For those of you playing along from another country, that's a mini version of Australia's Parliament House, which was designed by Italian architect Romaldo Giurgola. Urban legend says the occupant of this house worked on the big version.

035 *Essendon, Victoria*

Big love to green glass blocks, a monobrow and the most excellent gate. This street won a 'best kept pretty streets award' thing.

037 Newcastle, New South Wales

'Does your place have a view?'

'Yeah, but only of the ocean.'

038 Pascoe Vale South, Victoria

A super close-up was required because it's so lovely.

I was on the wireless talking about the differences between Sydney and Melbourne houses – that ole chestnut. So many similarities. So many differences. For one, I haven't found as many of these wrought-iron beauties in Sydney. It's entirely possible I'm staggering round the wrong suburbs though.

039 *Geelong, Victoria*

Black and white and beautiful in Geelong.

040 *Bellevue Hill, New South Wales*

Start each day with your own red-carpet moment.

041 *Clemton Park, New South Wales*

I don't do churches, but if I did, I'd do this one, because damn sure this is an Accidentally Wes Anderson doozy.

042 *Dromana, Victoria*

It's hard for me to take an original snap of the McCraith House, AKA the Butterfly House, AKA Larrakeyah, AKA Holy 💩. Take. A. Look. At. That.

Images don't really do it justice. Commissioned in 1954, completed in 1956, it commands its street and makes the other houses look a bit plain, including the one over the road designed by the same architecture firm, Chancellor and Patrick. It's about an hour's drive from Melbourne CBD. I'm calling it a Traffic-Stopper.

043 *The Entrance, New South Wales*

I wonder if this cutie started life as a holiday house or a forever home. Either way, I think it has seen some happy days – and, bravo, it's still standing. I'm calling it Survivalist Architecture.

044 *Kogarah, New South Wales*

So many lines. It looks like the house was dropped and put back together, Humpty-Dumpty style.

045 *Rosebud, Victoria*

I went to Rosebud with my lovely friends, had the most extraordinary sandwich with bacon and mango chutney, and managed to find this ace Fred-Flintstone-meets-Art-Deco-in-a-Romantic-way house.

046 *Albury, New South Wales*

It's important to bring your
A (frame) game on Saturdays.

047 *Toorak, Victoria*

This awkward pic is my attempt to capture a curvaceous concrete cantilevered staircase that's sitting near fab crazy paving, interesting windows and some awesome wrought iron.

048 Sans Souci, New South Wales

When I was a kid, I thought Sans Souci sounded like a very glamorous place to live.

049 East Melbourne, Victoria

I think this has a NOLA vibe. Not that I've been there.

050 *Ramsgate,*
New South Wales

'A smile is a curve that sets everything straight.'
– Phyllis Diller

051 *Canberra, Australian Capital Territory*

I'd blast out Herb Alpert on that patio and do a little dancing.

Designed in the 50s, finished in the 60s. The architect is JC Fitzgerald.

052 *Rose Bay, New South Wales*

Architect Douglas Forsyth Evans has been described as 'entrepreneurial' and 'bohemian' (the B-word thanks to his friendship with painter Norman Lindsay). The Chilterns is a Speculative apartment building by Evans with a cantilevered structural system, built 1953–54.

053 *Royston Park, South Australia*

Built in the 60s with a mid-century flavour, a Deco curve, some barley twists, cracking wrought iron and stone features. It's a bonza-mish-mash.

054 *Yass, New South Wales*

You might recognise this epic house from a 2016 episode of *Selling Houses Australia.*

Old Linton was built in 1857 and it's a biggie – you can sit fifty of your closest friends at the dining-room table, then most of them can sleep over. It's quite the architectural soup, built in the Federation Free Style with Art Deco bathrooms and Art Nouveau windows.

Fun fact: it was the first house in Yass to have electricity, gas and a telephone.

055 *Arncliffe, New South Wales*

This super-dooper house was built in 1977 by a young couple who worked closely with their Spanish architect on every detail, inside and out. It's a lovely story. As soon as I stopped, the delightful owner came out and told me about her house. I was gushing like a kid in the showbag hall.

056 *Ashgrove, Queensland*

I love a Top Cat yellow and purple combo.

057 Queanbeyan, New South Wales

Who knew there was so much cool in Queanbeyan? Also, who else has been spelling Queanbeyan incorrectly since forever?

059 *Mont Albert, Victoria*

This waterfall wonder, designed by Malcolm Langdon, has been hiding in its cul-de-sac since 1946.

Fun fact: 'Cul-de-sac' comes from French that literally means 'bottom of the bag' or 'bottom of the sack'.

058 *Wangaratta, Victoria*

'A crown is merely a hat that lets the rain in.' – Frederick the Great

060 Woollahra, New South Wales

I'm surprised this street corner isn't an accident blackspot. Wowsers! The architect is Oswald Deomede.

061 *Kew, Victoria*

Oh, clutch my pearls, that brickwork above the door! And the little round window! If only all doors could be this striking.

062 *Goulburn, New South Wales*

This town is a whole lot more than eating a pie while looking up a sheep's clacker.

064 *Balmain, New South Wales*

'Which one's yours?'

'The yellow one.'

'Yeah, but what's the street number?'

'It's the yellow one.'

063 *Sunshine, Victoria*

My new favourite suburb is living up to its name.

065 Glen Iris, Victoria

Sad face.

Mascara running.

Bags under the eyes.

066 Hamlyn Heights, Victoria

Another one for you letterbox lovers, from the most tremendous street in Geelong. How 'bout that wall? How 'bout that car?

067 Bendigo, Victoria

Oh. My.

It's Roseview, designed by Godfrey Eastorne, constructed in 1939 and sitting on Bendigo's main drag. It's hard to get the whole kit and caboodle of fabulousness in one pic, so I've started at the front gate, which has more style than my whole house.

068 *Dee Why, New South Wales*

Here's a delightfully colourful, slightly confused building with a shell on its forehead.

069 *Ascot Vale, Victoria*

Delicately enclosed.

070 Manly, New South Wales

I was fascinated by this building as a kid. It's sooooo glam, I was sure it was filled with jetsetters and TV gameshow hostesses.

Fun fact: the Bee Gees' song 'Kilburn Towers' is about this curvy beauty.

071 Mayfield, New South Wales

'Have you got a view from your place?'

'Yeah, but it's pretty cactus.'

072 Coburg North, Victoria

I think this sunroom would be even better in the rain.

073 Kingsford, New South Wales

This is the rear view. The front isn't as lovely. My dad would have called this 'the tradesman's entrance'.

074 Bundanoon, New South Wales

Started in 1896, completed in 1898, this building looks nothing like the rest of the village. It started life as Nicholas Golden Cross Ointment and Pill Factory, which produced a range of medicinal products including powders for 'female ailments'. It has also been a guest house and a German restaurant. Now it's The Pill Factory; it's very cool inside, and you can stay in it.

075 West Footscray, Victoria

Built by engineer James Montgomery and his family in 1960, featured by *The Design Files*, voted the best balcony for a dry martini (by me) and singularly responsible for increasing the cool levels in West Footscray.

076 *Beaufort, Victoria*

I see a chimney smiling at me
– a Kewpie doll, Mr Squiggle,
an eye roll, a winking minx,
a blonde vampire bat,
Thomas the Tank Engine,
a scary clown and the work
of an architect who likes
windows in chimneys.

077 Arncliffe, New South Wales

The combo of the front door, the angled cut-hole side-detail thing and the minty tone makes for a humble Aussie winner.

078 *Coburg, Victoria*

Captured here on a murky ole day, Villa Italia is an absolute heart-stopper. The 74-year-old beauty puts us to shame. She's currently getting a careful, Nonna-worthy revamp from her talented, passionate owners.

079 *Wombarra, New South Wales*

'You're so square, baby, I don't care.'
– Elvis Presley

080 *Carlton North, Victoria*

Twins. Fraternal, obvs.

081 *Earlwood, New South Wales*

With a dedication to Halloween, this gorgeous house is an Earlwood fave. It's a mid-40s building with an interesting mix of styles that add up to quite the urban fairytale. I'm partial to a super catslide roof, and after finding out the inside has P&O styling, I declare I'm smitten. The owners seem very nice, so I'm sure they won't mind some sharing arrangement.

082 Preston, Victoria

Preston – where eagles soar.

083 Coogee, New South Wales

The famous Coogee flatiron building. It's most famous for many people never actually noticing the unusual shape since it was built in the 1940s.

084 *Dee Why, New South Wales*

I see a smile with a missing tooth.

085 Princes Hill, Victoria

'In every house, when the curtains are drawn, there's a story going on, and you never get to hear.' – Peter Jackson

086 *Bar Beach, New South Wales*

Yes, there are two cannons on the corners. And a really terrific door. And super stonework. And heaps of cameras.

087 *St Kilda, Victoria*

The St Kilda style icon Sun-Blest. Built in 1860-ish; elegantly faded.

088 *Lake Wendouree, Victoria*

Herbert Leslie Coburns: Salome.

Mr Coburn practised architecture in his hometown of Ballarat from 1905 to 1956.

089 *Warrawong, New South Wales*

It's the WTAF half-house. I believe there are three half-houses in the area. What's going on in the Gong – commitment issues?

090 Caulfield North, Victoria

From the pebbled path to the metal-grille screen door, this razzle-dazzler is square in the best possible way. I'm imagining all the folks standing on the terrazzo tiles at the front door about to enter for a night soundtracked by Burt Bacharach. Designed by Polish-born architect Bernard Slawik, it was built in 1963–64 and has a statement of significance on it from the local council thanks to its Modernist aesthetic. I couldn't walk on by.

091 *Annandale,*
New South Wales

Confectionary style.

092 *Coburg, Victoria*

Despite being slightly unsettled by the scary bitey-faced plant at Villa Gissarra, I do love a garden with a sense of humour. Thanks to all you wacky funsters out there with your hedgers and stick-on eyes.

093 Balmain, New South Wales

I doubt this place has ever had that dreary Monday mood.

094 Safety Beach, Victoria

Tourists were not partial to swimming in Shark Bay, so the name was changed to Safety Beach. True story.

095 *Fawkner, Victoria*

Some of the first European settlers in Fawkner were a Mr Michael Dowling and his family, including a Miss Dowling who described the area as 'a harsh windy place with a few trees and a few unfinished shacks'. This is entirely inaccurate now. Fawkner is filled with well-manicured front yards, clean curvy windows, bloody lovely wrought iron and a fabulous old-school bakery.

096 Canowindra, New South Wales

Known primarily for bush rangers and the interesting pronunciation of its name, Canowindra has a bangin' main drag.

097 Wangaratta, Victoria

S is for 'special'. Which describes this house and Wangaratta perfectly. If you can take your eyes off the beautiful clinker brick features, squint for a look at the most divine little stained-glass windows.

098 *Bankstown, New South Wales*

Magnificence surrounds us, sitting quietly in a Bankstown street, looking suspiciously like the work of Gino Volpato. The architect's family has confirmed that this is one of his: another Volpato tracked down and recorded. For the dedicated such as myself, the hunt continues. Like an architecture lover's Easter Egg hunt.

099 Sunshine, Victoria

'Anything is possible with sunshine and a little pink.'
– Lilly Pulitzer

100 *Fairfield, New South Wales*

Cruising, Fairfield-style. Let's hold this house up as a top five in Survivalist Architecture. I'd guess it was built in the 50s, and I'd guess it once had some similarly styled mates nearby. That concrete wall is built to last – or maybe nobody with my reversing skills has ever lived here.

101 *Goulburn, New South Wales*

Who doesn't love orange trim with concrete stairs and a stone feature wall? Built in 1956–57 by the architectural team Brown and Brewer, this statement house is heritage listed as 'DWELLING'. Which is informative. It hasn't been for sale since ever, so I reckon the original stone-loving folks are still here.

102 *Golden Point, Victoria*

This area was known as Poverty Point until a bit of Au (gold) was found in 1851. In 1970, Sovereign Hill open-air museum was built nearby, a recreation of the original Golden Point settlement. Anyhoo, this house is a darling.

103 *Thomastown, Victoria*

After spending the week trimming the hedge Torana and washing the Commodore, it's time to get the money's worth out of those shutters with a nanna nap.

104 Double Bay,
New South Wales

Imagine standing on that terrific little balcony, listening to Glenn Miller, sipping an adult beverage, looking over Sydney Harbour and contemplating the newish bridge, wishing you'd put a quid on that Kiwi Phar Lap.

105 *Beaumaris, Victoria*

This is The Nagel House, a 1957 Daniel Wheeler design that's been beautifully renovated and extended. How 'bout that Monaro?

Fun fact: Beaumaris Modern opens selected houses each year so you can go *inside* to see the tremendousness rather than just standing out the front dribbling.

106 Sandringham, New South Wales

A Bedrock-vibe front entrance in Sandringham.

107 North Melbourne, Victoria

Paris in North Melbourne. Who needs to fuss around with flying?

108 *Merewether, New South Wales*

The angle on those windows! Sitting on its beautiful brickwork, looking over Merewether, this 1950s house has one of my top-ten sunrooms.

109 Rockdale, New South Wales

Current mood – droopy.

Fun fact: I love it when nice folks suggest houses for me to look at. One of those nice folks was very surprised when I posted a pic of their house – this one. Which they didn't suggest. Which I found randomly. That was a little bit spooky.

110 Bendigo, Victoria

The current owners of this house, which was built in 1953, have been here since '98 and were in the front yard.

'May I take a picture of your beautiful house please?'

'You certainly may.'

'You know its design is based on a ship?'

'I do.'

'I'd rather be in your house than on a ship though.'

'Me too,' said the lovely owner.

111 Maroubra, New South Wales

It's smiling. I'd smile too if I was a yellow combo render-and-board cottage with matching striped awnings, cool wrought iron and *the* most divine tiled path.

112 *Caulfield North, Victoria*

Not being a native Victorian, I ask for potato scallops, always look both ways before I get off the tram and usually have no idea what's around the corner. Like this. In a quiet street – *boom*. Labassa is one of Australia's most outstanding 19th-century mansions. It was home to Hollywood's first Australian silent film star, Louise Lovely. It's a National Trust of Victoria building, so you can go see it for yourself.

113 Earlwood, New South Wales

I see a face, eyebrows and a sideways baseball cap. And a garage door with a palm tree.

114 *Retro garage doors*

They might be a total bugger to open, but who cares – they look cool.

115 *Black Rock, Victoria*

Taking seaside shacks to dizzying heights, Saade House was built in 1975 for a Lebanese family, designed by the masters of meticulous glamour, Polish architects Helen and John Holgar.

I was on the outside. I checked out some recent pics on Domain for an inside sticky beak. The house has an extraordinary interior, including a staircase so remarkable that dramatic music should be played when anyone descends.

116 *Kingsford, New South Wales*

Colours and curves with a cherry on top.

117 *South Yarra, Victoria*

This house is looking at me like
I'm a bad smell.

118 *New Lambton Heights, New South Wales*

Sometimes you can't see the forest for the trees, or the stucco house for the polychrome caps on the front wall.

120 *Kew, Victoria*

It's beautifully square; it's Robin Boyd. It's a child of the late 60s.

The Lawrence House and Flat is in Studley Park, an area rich with significant post-war houses and streets of dramatic Modernist architecture. A who's who of Australian architects can be found in Kew.

119 *Forestville, South Australia*

Solid and sleepy.

121 Carlton North, Victoria

Mum's sister and her husband might be a bit shabby, but they can still keep a beady eye on you. Neighbourhood watch: Victorian edition.

122 Narrabundah, Australian Capital Territory

Doesn't that look like the sunniest place for a cuppa?

Designed in 1959 by local Canberra architect JC Fitzgerald, this Modernist beauty has only had three owners in sixty-three years.

The big windows on the street prove that Modernist architecture lovers find privacy ridiculously overrated.

I'd be so chuffed to sit in the sun, admiring all the house's tremendous features with the lovely and lucky owner.

123 Richmond, Victoria

'You've gotta be a caterpillar before you can be a butterfly. Problem is, most people aren't willing to be a caterpillar.' – Anonymous

124 *Botany, New South Wales*

A sneaky peek over the fence. Oooh aaaah, a post-war stunner with an oasis vibe. Sometimes I get irrationally cross at plants that hide the houses, but in this case I'll accept it.

125 Templestowe, Victoria

I wonder if anyone in this house has that Sunday-night, haven't-done-my-homework feeling?

I left school when Dead or Alive were in the top ten, but still get a ripple of anxiety when I hear the tick-tick-tick of *60 Minutes* … uh-oh, time to start that essay.

126 Wingello, New South Wales

This country cutie is a survivor; it's tougher than it looks. Fire rampaged through Wingello in the summer of 2019/2020 and homes were destroyed – not for the first time, either. Wingello has known fires before.

If you are passing through, do stop for a good coffee, the greatest hamburgers and some mixed lollies. There's only one shop; you'd be a dill to miss it.

127 Bondi, New South Wales

Mesopotamian style. It's quite fancy in some parts of Bondi. I do love it when you can actually see a person's hobby.

128 Moorooka, Queensland

I'm loving the sharpness of this 70s beauty in Moorooka.

I'm also loving the Copper Art house sign.

129 South Yarra, Victoria

'Pink isn't just a colour. It's an attitude too.' – Miley Cyrus

130 *Sydney, New South Wales*

Ah, regarde. Ça alors, ce truc est chouette.

131 *Long Jetty, New South Wales*

I bet this is not what springs to mind when someone says Long Jetty to you. Personally, I always think of INXS, because they played at the legendary Long Jetty Hotel in '82 and I desperately wanted to go.

132 *Brunswick West, Victoria*

'Make it look like a tree trunk. We went to Yosemite on a tour bus and just love trees.'

133 *Maroubra, New South Wales*

Thwarted by a most inconveniently placed bus stop, I present this oddly angled pic of a masterpiece of breezeblocks. And tiles. And a funky fence.

134 *Grange, South Australia*

The Deco crazy paving combo was a lot to take in, then the etchings in the windows tipped me over the edge. This was built in the mid-50s, and I'm saying masterpiece.

135 *East Melbourne, Victoria*

If I can't have a divine Deco apartment, then I'd like one of these, please. I'm loving the decent-sized balconies (thanks to the thoughtfulness of 1950s design), but most of all I'd love to have that glassed-in staircase so I could take in the view as I climbed – to distract me from my huffing and puffing.

136 *Goulburn, New South Wales*

Goulburn has quite the variety of architectural styles. If you have a thing for Egyptian-looking stuff, then here you go. If you have a thing for coloured glazed polychrome terracotta, then you'd know this was one of the first buildings in Australia to use it. Built between 1933 and 1935, the Elmslea Chambers also has Art Deco sunbursts, cute bird motifs and a lovely soft-pink hue.

137 *Mosman, New South Wales*

Mosman homes are quite hard to snap, as the front-garden and big-fence games are strong.

138 *Rosebud, Victoria*

It's just so stinking cute. I can hear my mum saying, 'Don't you dare touch that fish fern.' Pulling off the fronds and putting them down my brother's shirt was a childhood highlight for me. That, my young friends, is how we amused ourselves before mobile phones.

Back to the stinkin' cute house – look at the wood detail under the roofline.

139 Elwood, Victoria

The design on this gate reminds me of that bridge in London. You know the one – the parapet casts a vulgar shadow onto the ground at a certain time of day. It has been amusing mature Australians like me for years.

140 Burwood, New South Wales

Pick me, pick me, pick me …

141 *East Lindfield, New South Wales*

Before you ask, no, I haven't mucked around with filters – it really is margarine-yellow. It was completed in 1941 for the then-Meadow Lea Margarine Company sales manager, James Armstrong. Meadow Lea House, East Lindfield. Yes, that's its actual name.

142 *Templestowe, Victoria*

Super shiny, slick 70s glamour in Templestowe; a Holgar and Holgar gem. I wanted to get closer to the famous front door, but who wants a random nuisance soggy stranger at close range? John Holgar and Helen Holgar were responsible for some of the coolest Australian homes from the mid-60s to the mid-90s.

143 Dover Heights, New South Wales

That time I stumbled upon the *Love My Way* house, relived the sad bit, and had to have a Bex and a lie-down.

144 Brunswick, Victoria

I've got balcony and garage door envy.

145 *Wagga Wagga, New South Wales*

Symmetry is all fun and games until someone moves the bird bath.

146 *Coburg North, Victoria*

When letterboxes attack.

147 *Arncliffe, New South Wales*

I've got that Visage song in my head. It reminds me of Macao. Random, perhaps, but if you've been there you might get my drift.

148 Essendon, Victoria

It's not a washing line, it's a halo.

149 Richmond, Victoria

When I was an ankle biter, Halloween was something important to Samantha in *Bewitched*. If you know Richmond in Melbourne, you know this place is 24/7 spooky. The owner isn't actually interested in the 31st of October; he invited me inside for a tour and a chat.

Fact: the inside is more interesting than the outside, and the outside is magnificent.

150 Mount Ousley, New South Wales

If it hadn't been such a grey ole day, I would have been blinded by the white. It's so wonderfully crisp. I think the plants are bowing to the house in a 'we are not worthy' way.

151 *South Yarra, Victoria*

'Gate' may have become the syllable of scandal, from Watergate to Nipplegate, but this no-nonsense square block would be incapable of any such thing.

152 *Bateau Bay, New South Wales*

Who wants to go to this almost-A-frame for some leaf raking and a game of Hungry Hungry Hippos? This is a swinging 70s model. The first A-frames were built in California as lakeside holiday houses. This bottler is a short stroll to the beach.

153 Coogee, New South Wales

Non-stop glamour in the Hollywood end of Coogee.

154 *Goulburn, New South Wales*

I screen, you screen, we all scream for that screen.

155 St Kilda East, Victoria

From the succulent-edged pond to the asymmetrical crown, the clinker bricks, that highlight above the entrance and that long, lean window in the round bit, this 1930s palace was almost worth the hideous driving manoeuvre I did when I spotted it.

156 Lugarno, New South Wales

Lovely in Lugarno just rolls off my tongue.

Fun fact: According to a 2012 survey conducted by the governments of Australia and New Zealand, Lugarno has the most roundabouts per capita in the southern hemisphere – slightly beating the Victorian town of Sausage Gully.

157 *Topiary*

Tow-pee-uh-ree

Tow-pie-uh-ree

Either way, it's clipped balls.

158 Woollahra, New South Wales

These twin sweeties have badges on them: 'Register of the National Estate Historic Plaques Program Woollahra Municipal Council Terrace House for Front Fencing'.

A few of you will be excited by the unusual Flemish Gable; others will be more impressed that there are no cars or bins out the front.

Some websites note the date of construction as 1890; others 1900. What's ten years between friends?

159 *Coburg, Victoria*

I've got chimney envy. I want a wine-bottle-shaped chimney made of bricks.

161 Bellevue Hill, New South Wales

This house was built in 1937 for the Provost family, and the architect is Sydney Ancher. Described as the first functionally designed house in Australia, it was lucky to escape the wreckers in 1989. The stated reasons for demolition included that the sunroom was too small, the garage access inconvenient and the open decks too exposed to the public. The Land and Environment Court ruled that the house was an ace example of radical International Style and said no to demolition. So, thankfully, we can still stand out the front and go *ooooooh*.

160 Canada Bay, New South Wales

This is, of course, a home designed by the one and only Mr Gino Volpato. I'm crushing hard on the front door and letterbox and tiles. I love everything about it, except that it's not mine and I don't live near it.

162 *Tootgarook, Victoria*

Seeing is believing.

The Tootgarook Parthenon.

163 *Dee Why, New South Wales*

The driveway game is strong here.

Things Northern Beaches people love: the Sea Eagles, driveways, Lucky & Peps, hiding the houses behind shrubs, carports, telling people they saw The Oils at The Antler.

Things they don't love: crossing bridges.

164 Prahran, Victoria

In a world full of grey …

165 *Kew, Victoria*

It's all fun and games until you stack it in your nanna undies and end up on YouTube.

166 Mordialloc, Victoria

It looks like a cranky squinting king with a Basquiat crown.

167 Arncliffe, New South Wales

Grand in a 3D, 'hey what is that, pull over' kind of way, this is a 1970s Gino Volpato.

168 *Ararat, Victoria*

Big skies and big features are a thing in Ararat. My fave parts are the decorative concrete pretend balcony bits.

169 *Banksia, New South Wales*

Upstairs downstairs.

170 *Moss Vale, New South Wales*

Not all country houses are cute'n'cuddly.

171 Carlton North, Victoria

Same same, but different.

172 East Lindfield, New South Wales

If I was a kid, I'd call this a princess house.

173 Leichhardt, New South Wales

A high forehead is a sign of intelligence.

174 *Thirroul, New South Wales*

Not even the 💩 weather could distract from the wonderfulness of that wall. Oh, now I've got that Oasis song stuck in my head.

175 *Clifton Hill, Victoria*

If I'm gonna eat this stuff, I do it in great style.

176 Pearl Beach, New South Wales

Rockmelon and fancy blocks.

177 Collaroy, New South Wales

So close to being black and white at Number 9.

178 *Parkville, Victoria*

I love Parkville. I love its name, and I love pottering around here because I never know what I'm going to find next – like this little sweetie that looks like a flatiron that's been sat on.

179 *Queanbeyan, New South Wales*

Queanbeyan, a place best known for being where the booze was when Canberra was dry and as a source of both kinds of rugby players. Who knew all this retro cool was there?

180 *Glebe, New South Wales*

Carcoar? Collector? Taralga? Rugby? Gunning?

Nah. Inner-city Sydney.

181 *Kew East, Victoria*

Designed by architect Keith Lodge, when he was in his mid-twenties, this magic house was his much-loved family home until recently. Completed in 1959, Lodge House is an example of the Modernist movement, and it has been classified by the National Trust of Australia (Victoria) as being of regional significance.

It sits in a beautiful garden, so this is the best pic I could get without annoying anyone.

182 Palm Beach, New South Wales

'I sat in a garage and invented the future.' – Steve Jobs

I doubt very much it was this garage, as the view would be waaaaaay too distracting.

183 *Dulwich Hill, New South Wales*

I could look at this all day. It looks content and totally comfortable in its own skin.

184 *Reservoir, Victoria*

What lovely curves you have. I'm certainly resembling this house after the two-year Covid carbohydrate feast.

185 *Manly, New South Wales*

Split nationalities.

186 *Earlwood, New South Wales*

Looking out over a quiet street in super-suburbia, this is an attention-grabbing suburban symphony. It's a beautiful castle from dream creator Gino Volpato.

187 Princes Hill, Victoria

In your best Darryl Kerrigan voice:
'What do you call that, darl?'

188 *Kirribilli, New South Wales*

'How's the view from your new place?'

'Well, it's hardly Venice, but we cope.'

189 *Sunshine, Victoria*

Stop right here.

Bondi?

Elwood?

St Kilda?

Nah, 1930s-built divine Deco in Sunshine.

190 *Kiama, New South Wales*

Fun fact: Orry George Kelly, who won three Oscars for Best Costume Design in the 1950s, was born in Kiama. This house, while super stylish like Orry-Kelly, has nothing to do with him at all.

191 Caulfield North, Victoria

Copper – Cu.

193 *Cronulla, New South Wales*

'How you goin', Mr Vickers – getting heaps?'

Before those of you of a certain age get too excited, that's not the house Debbie lived in in the movie. That's in Port Hacking.

And the house from the TV series (*Puberty Blues*) was drastically remodelled.

192 *Cobram, Victoria*

Curved windows + wrought iron + that balcony + crazy paving = ring-a-ding-ding.

194 Camberwell, Victoria

Between the weather and the Golf Links Estate, I'd swear I was in jolly old England. The Riversdale Golf Club was subdivided in 1927 and the first houses were built in 1928, with the majority occupied by 1938.

Fun fact: Barry Humphries's father, Eric, was a builder and constructed eighteen of the houses. Have a lovely day, possums.

195 Caulfield North, Victoria

I feel like I got a bit cooler just standing near this.

This ripper was erected in 1972–73 for a Cypriot-born cinema magnate and his wife, to a design from the Polish husband-and-wife team Holgar and Holgar.

196 *St Kilda East, Victoria*

I was standing at the driveway entrance when the owner came home and told me about his house. It's three apartments. His is the whole ground floor – 34 square metres – and it's still completely original. Construction started in 1932 and finished in 1934, and you might recognise the building from various TV shows and movies, including a role as Shirley Temple's first Hollywood home in an Australian-filmed biopic. The owner had some absolutely fascinating stories, including some *Underbelly* stuff I thought best not to retell here. There's a series in this house.

197 Letterboxes

'Nothing echoes like an empty mailbox.' – Charles M Schulz

198 *Geelong, Victoria*

This is exactly the kind of house I used to think my nanna should live in, with bakelite containers of Iced VoVos, a teapot with a cute cosy and *My Fair Lady* playing on the radiogram.

199 *Castlecrag, New South Wales*

It's almost too much for one frame. The Mercer House was built in 1940 and designed by Eric Nicholls, an associate of Walter Burley Griffin.

Originally single-storey, the house had a second storey added to it in the early 50s. It's got such a golden Jean Harlow glow about it.

200 Bendigo, Victoria

Door. Stained glass. Wrought iron.
Red slate roof. Circular awning thing.
Round door bit. Decorative concrete.
Metal awning. Art Nouveau details.
Take your time.

201 Austinmer, New South Wales

The house is extraordinary. This pic is not.

Is that a haiku?

Built in 1945, it's salmon coloured, both square and curvy, beautifully painted, delightfully cactus'ed and in great nick.

202 Fitzroy North, Victoria

I've had shingles. It was quite uncomfortable. I didn't have a happy 🐝 to cheer me up. This is One Mani House; it's quirky and a welcome, smile-inducing Melbourne favourite.

203 Goulburn, New South Wales

This window. And that stonework. It's so out there – I think I love it ...? I'm not actually sure.

204 *St Kilda East, Victoria*

Good morning from houses that look like ducks. Hopefully those little quacks aren't structural.

205 *Pymble, New South Wales*

Bold and curved in all the right places, with beautiful pebble-crete, bespoke glass and brick artistry, this house is solid as a rock but oh so delicate. It's Gino Volpato's distinctive art adding magnificence to Sydney's Upper North Shore. In my opinion, it's a welcome style boost to the area.

206 *Curl Curl, New South Wales*

'Gimme a home …' Sorry not sorry: that's stuck in your head now.

207 Ararat, Victoria

Welcome. Take a seat in the good lounge. Can I get you a Resch's Dinner Ale?

208 Elwood, Victoria

The Elwood streets, named after notable old dead poets, are now the home of modern poets, beloved Australian singer-songwriters, playwrights and assorted creatives.

209 Lyneham, Australian Capital Territory

'The hardest thing about living in Canberra is that almost everyone who doesn't love here asks: Why on earth would you live in Canberra? Loudly, and in a way they would never use to discuss anywhere else. And they would never listen.' – Judy Horacek

I'm with Judy. I love Canberra.

210 Woollahra, New South Wales

I love seeing horns on a building.

211 *Robertson, New South Wales*

Saddle my horse, I'm off to Robertson.

Robertson – home of the Big Poo, Miriam Margolyes and this castle.

212 *Preston, Victoria*

Does anyone else see ballerinas bending over?

213 *Queenscliff, Victoria*

It was a grim grey day when I went to Queenscliff, but this wooden lovely and the free stuff out the front warmed my cold heart.

214 *Sylvania Waters, New South Wales*

If this house was mine, I'd turn that excellent concrete bench around and spend my days admiring my bricks.

215 Bondi, New South Wales

You know, Bondi isn't all Deco, white-glass palaces and buildings avoiding demolition to make more glass palaces. This bit of the hood is so Spanish Mission, it's as if I've been to California.

216 Maryborough, Victoria

Country goals.

217 *Murrumbeena, Victoria*

What year was this built?

Interweb says 1975.

Survey says … Nah.

218 *Coburg, Victoria*

From the front, this mostly makes sense. From the side, not so much.

219 *Potts Point, New South Wales*

At the time of completion in 1936, Wyldefel Gardens was considered the most modern example of residential architecture in Australia. It's a reclusive member of Potts Point, a well-known and well-kept secret.

Socialite philanthropist and art collector William Crowle, in collaboration with architect John Brogan, created this beautiful Continental Modern haven with a Sydney Harbour frontage. Sadly, the complex lost its billion-dollar view, tennis court and swimming pool in the 40s, when the Navy reclaimed the waterfront to build Garden Island. Mr Crowle relocated his house and boat across the harbour to Kurraba Point (see *268*).

220 *Goulburn, New South Wales*

If you are going to do statues, go hard or go home.

222 *West End, Queensland*

Considered to be Australia's most iconic style, the Queenslander is also the most deceptive, by looking like a two-storey house. With their deep verandas and shutters, they look as cool as the beer you would be offered when you arrived.

221 *Balmain, New South Wales*

Framed.

223 Glenelg East, South Australia

There are five places in Australia with palindromic names.

There are four places called Glenelg in the world.

224 Gosford, New South Wales

Starting life as a funeral parlour, this building has been a few things since it was constructed in 1930, including the object of a hard-fought battle for survival. It's my understanding that it's safe now. And it's a bar. Happy dance.

225 Robertson, New South Wales

Clipped balls in Robertson. This is where *Babe* was filmed, and a fence on this property was in the movie. Star struck. Would you be surprised to learn that *Babe* caused a huge spike in vegetarianism? *La la laa.*

226 Camberwell, Victoria

I do not know the correct term for that double-split-looking conjoined-twin chimney.

So I will just leave it at ...

- cat slide
- so many bricks
- clinker bricks
- steeply pitched, easy-to-fall-off roof.

227 Earlwood, New South Wales

If you are an Earlwoodian, you will know the building is actually this colour and actually this shape. It has got an Ettamogah Pub meets Dr Seuss feel to it.

228 *Ivanhoe East, Victoria*

On the paddddeeeeeeoooo we surely sit.

229 *Manly, New South Wales*

Lizard scale brickwork.

230 *Queanbeyan, New South Wales*

I do like a matchy-matchy mini-me letterbox.

And flat roofs.

And spiky pergolas.

And weatherboards.

And blue trim.

And stonework.

And a wee bit of shabbiness.

231 *Magill, South Australia*

Shiny pointy places to read in or pretend you are in a ski chalet.

232 *St Kilda East, Victoria*

Turns out houses can say howdy.

233 *Northcote, Victoria*

You know when kittens are so cute you want to nibble on them? I feel the same way about this house.

234 Merewether, New South Wales

I walked a country mile looking for this Ross Deamer-designed house. I wasn't disappointed; it's as gorgeous as I was expecting.

235 *Travancore, Victoria*

If this was my place, I'm not sure what would make me happier:

- that front door
- the Krusty-tribute brick feature
- the bricks that look like a ladder
- the location
- the curved concrete awning.

236 *Reservoir, Victoria*

A fountain can be described as a decorative reservoir for discharging water.

237 *Surfboard letterboxes*

Duke Kahanamoku was a Hawaiian Olympian swimmer who popularised surfing as an international sport. He visited Sydney in 1915, made a surfboard from a tree and taught his sport to the locals. This was not what he had in mind for the future of surfboards in Australia.

238 *Bondi, New South Wales*

I read that we love curves because they relate more closely to the human form.

239 *Beaumaris, Victoria*

Some see well-behaved ivy, some see *Saturday Night Fever.*

240 *Highfields, New South Wales*

How 'bout this:

- ✓ flat roof
- ✓ cool, resortish-style foliage
- ✓ great use of tiles
- ✓ breezeblocks … double tick
- ✓ love love love the green trim
- ✓ elegant wrought iron
- ✓ a lawn that would make my dad jealous.

241 *South Yarra, Victoria*

I love how much is going on here. A few houses down, a lady asked what I was doing then offered me her car space. What's also going on here is lovely manners.

242 *Footscray, Victoria*

Time Out magazine placed Footscray at 13th in its '50 Coolest neighbourhoods in the World' list for 2019. I think this smoking-hot doozy was a contributing factor.

243 Merrylands West, New South Wales

I was surprised there was no one on the patio admiring that lawn. If it was mine, I'd sell tickets.

244 *Ascot Vale, Victoria*

Please don't sit on the wall.

245 *Goulburn, New South Wales*

Built by a man who was transported for life and then freed, this house has also been a saddlery and an inn. Any one of the owners could be responsible for the window and symmetry crimes.

246 *Beacon Hill, New South Wales*

All quiet on the hill. The mowing was done yesterday, so today's agenda includes a quick spin around The Mall before not watching any footy on the telly.

247 West Footscray, Victoria

There is too much swoon-ness here for a whole house shot, so let's focus:

- the honey-coloured bricks
- the cool tile feature on the chimney
- the gate
- OMG the gate
- the wrought-iron entrance
- big beautiful side windows
- the black-edge tile on the front door
- the cat-slide thing on the chimney.

248 Bondi, New South Wales

If Barbie was a Sydney girl ...

249 Little Bay, New South Wales

This looks more like suburban London than seaside Sydney.

Like many of the buildings in Little Bay, this 1920 Deco beauty started life as part of Prince Henry Hospital, which served as New South Wales's first hospital for infectious diseases from 1881 to 2003. There is the most marvellous museum nearby.

The friendly locals tell me this building was a kids' ward, that it's allegedly haunted and that monkeys were kept here. Now it's apartments.

Fun fact: Little Bay is the beach that artists Christo and Jeanne-Claude wrapped in plastic in 1968–69.

250 *Brunswick East, Victoria*

Who knows what it's hiding? A weak chin?

251 *Preston, Victoria*

We can run Tudor Revival bingo on this gem, 'Le Chateau' on aptly named Diamond Street:

- recessed porch
- brick-edged windowsills
- tall chimney with fancy thing
- multiple front-facing gables
- cool decorative brick motifs
- round clock-looking thing
- brick corbelled eaves.

The only thing missing is a Mock Henry.

252 *Kogarah, New South Wales*

I nearly fell over and did myself a mischief when this appeared in its largely orange-brick suburb. A website tells me the design is based on the owner's memories – his childhood of fishing, kite-flying and folk music reinterpreted as sculpture in terracotta. The colour of the stonework sits very well with the orange bricks. Oh, listen to me being all Kevin McCloud.

The house is called Sabita, and I think it's just marvellous.

253 Bendigo, Victoria

Kettle's boiled. Jatz are on a plate.
Tupperware party starts at three.

254 Maroubra, New South Wales

Bone structure is everything.

255 Ararat, Victoria

Country monobrow.

256 *Burwood, New South Wales*

That's a statement-making entrance by statement master Gino Volpato.

257 *St Lucia, Queensland*

It's an A-frame, split chimney, Tudor-style combo with extra foliage – designed by Leo Joseph Drinan. Built in 1936, it's a charming example of interwar Modernism, intentionally different from the other joints being constructed at the same time.

258 Coburg, Victoria

The gate, the round window, the entrance, the paving, the house number, the awnings, the wall, that round bit above the entrance and the damn aircon unit. Love. It. All.

259 *Umina Beach, New South Wales*

If you are of a certain age, and if you were lucky, this is what summer looked like when you were a kid after your nanna moved up the coast to be near the new Masonic club.

260 *Randwick, New South Wales*

Rear views on Randwick. Taken lying down in the rain between the bins. No, I don't need any help getting up, but thanks.

261 *Ballarat, Victoria*

Trelawne, a Modern P&O-ship-style house far from the ocean. It's the work of architect Herbert Leslie Coburn for manufacturing magnate Herbert John Tippett, and it was completed in 1930.
Note:

- uncluttered attitude
- hard to get in one shot
- glass bricks you can't really see
- surprised expression.

262 Eden Hills, South Australia

'Sometimes it's best not to say anything but just sit, sigh and marvel.' – Anonymous

263 *Rye, Victoria*

It's so Palm Beach, it's a Rat Pack getaway.

264 *Burwood, New South Wales*

A castle is generally described as a medieval stronghold where kings or lords usually reside.

265 Caulfield North, Victoria

Completed in 1972–73, this is a European Modernist design from Holgar and Holgar with a unique Moorish-style vaulted arcade. It's Moorish, alright – more stylish, more glam, more cool, more everything.

266 *North Sydney, New South Wales*

These terrific flats are opposite St Leonards Park. As a kid, I was fascinated and terrified by a concrete tower that sat slap-bang in the middle of that park, which I was told was a sewerage pipe. I did think it was full of you-know-what. If it was in London, it would have been turned into a house and featured on *Grand Designs*.

267 *Daylesford, Victoria*

Plain and simple with a super ski-slope roof. There are a lot of notable people from Daylesford: must be something in the water.

268 Kurraba Point, New South Wales

Here's a Sydney waterfront legend. When I was a kid, we'd fish near this house, and Dad used to tell us it had been moved here on a boat from the mysterious other side of the harbour. We imagined the whole house on a boat and thought Dad was pulling our legs. Turns out, it's a true story. The house was originally part of Wyldefel Gardens in Potts Point and was designed by John Brogan in 1935 for the art collector William Crowle. In the 1940s, land reclamation meant his house and boatshed had to be demolished, so he moved the whole thing across the water on a barge, piece by piece.

269 Avalon, New South Wales

That's as close as I can get to the divine Alexander House without being a pest. This cool as a cucumber house has been an Avalon local since 1957.

270 Hamlyn Heights, Victoria

Looks like the first crown of the Baratheon dynasty.

272 *Goulburn, New South Wales*

Here's another corker from Australia's first inland city. What is it about round windows? It's a bit Modernist; some might say it's got a bit of Bauhaus. Like Goulburn, it's a mish-mash that works.

271 *Arncliffe, New South Wales*

Symmetrical sisters in their Victorian finery. And a pole.

273 *St Kilda, Victoria*

Curve-side appeal. Chelmer Lodge has been lurking elegantly just behind the main drag at St Kilda since the 30s. Featuring ...

- clinker bricks
- bonus contrasting clinker bricks
- extra-round overhanging thing
- solid no-loitering pointy-topped front wall
- generous curves
- nice-shaped pittosporum
- magnificent windows.

274 *Monterey, New South Wales*

'When in doubt, wear red.' – Bill Blass

276 *Rosebud, Victoria*

I'm quite confident that I'd look as relaxed as this place after a few public holidays here.

Did you know, Australia gets about half as many public holidays as Liechtenstein, but more than Mexico? Reading the list of public holidays by country is very interesting – even more so when in a holiday house.

275 *Kew, Victoria*

The stairway to retro heaven.

277 Ballarat, Victoria

I'm having a *Play School* moment with those windows.

278 Pascoe Vale South, Victoria

It's hip to be square.

279 Manly, New South Wales

Watching over the boats in the harbour since forever.

280 Toorak, Victoria

This was designed by Marcus Martin for Sir Hamilton Sleigh of the Golden Fleece petroleum family. It's 1934, heritage listed and breathtakingly white. I'm not sure whether I'm pleased or disappointed that sheep tributes were resisted in the design.

281 South Coogee, New South Wales

Cactus and pastels for a smile-inducing garage.

282 *Yarralumla, Australian Capital Territory*

Designed in 1953 and completed in 1954, this is the work of Kenneth Henry Bell Oliphant. A Bendigo lad by birth, Oliphant came to Canberra in the mid-1920s with architecture firm Oakley & Parkes. By 1930, he had designed more than thirty private houses, earning him recognition as one of Canberra's first private architects and a major influence in the Australian Capital Territory's domestic look. The butterfly roof is glorious. I insist you don't focus on the bins, and instead drool over those diamond windows and stonework.

283 South Yarra, Victoria

Who says Deco is all monobrows? Described as a landmark Art Deco design, York House is impressively manicured. I see a bride's bodice. Or a wedding cake. Or a giant doily. Or Nanna's toilet-roll dolly.

284 Bexley North, New South Wales

I just want to cartwheel right up to the front door. I'm sure that was Mr Volpato's intention when he finalised the design.

285 *Kew, Victoria*

Pretty in pink, isn't she?

286 Mount Ousley, New South Wales

When you take a good look, there's plenty going on here. I'm not sure what I love the most: the curved flat bit, the flat curved bit or the wave in the concrete awning.

287 *Parkville, Victoria*

I do love architecture inspired by confectionary. This is an edible collection of units and a townhouse, built in 1939.

288 *Carina, Queensland*

I'm going to require an explanation for this please.

289 *Horsham, Victoria*

Two words: screen door.

290 Capel Sound, Victoria

Here's Rose Maree, sitting behind her school fence, waiting for her weekend visitors to arrive and listen to Dire Straits.

291 Reservoir, Victoria

It's like double denim, but in brick.

292 *Caulfield North, Victoria*

The Aroona Road Modernist Precinct is four super-swinging houses in Caulfield North, all built between 1961 and 1971. Two are by Austrian architect Ernest Fooks, and two by Holgar and Holgar. All are European Modernist style. This geometric gem is one of the Holgar and Holgar designs, and it was ready for action in 1971.

293 *Queanbeyan, New South Wales*

White line fever.

294 *Bondi, New South Wales*

Not even a scruffy bush, a pesky non-matching car and a photobombing crane could dampen my enthusiasm for this curvy crowd-stopper.

295 Earlwood, New South Wales

Panels, pebble-crete, a flat roof, swimming-pool tiles and retro garage doors. It's a mid-century palace.

296 Albury, New South Wales

Thomas Richard Fielder, a bricklayer of note, came to Albury in 1927. Built in 1948, this house has his distinctive tapestry brick decorative touches front and centre. Responsible for some of Albury's finest buildings, Mr Fielder was referred to as 'an absolute artist'. He also worked in Canberra on The Lodge.

297 *East Melbourne, Victoria*

I like to imagine that the residents of these apartments are as ace as their building, all with martinis in hand and listening to Doris Day.

298 Mosman, New South Wales

The family who built this had a thing for citadels, having completed Innisfallen Castle in Castle Cove prior to this. It hardly seems fair that some people have multiple castles while I have none.

299 Bendigo, Victoria

Sleepy eyes.

300 Reservoir, Victoria

There are many things closed on a Sunday, none so much as this place. There is no roast on here, take a hint. Bye.

Acknowledgements

You very rarely get to say thank you to people in such a prominent way.

In no particular order but with my deepest gratitude, thanks to …

All the lovely people who let me stay in their homes so I could look at other people's.

All the lovely people who put up with me in a car. You know. I'm sorry.

Noah –what would I do without you telling me where to go and sharing your passion?

The Volpato family, always so generous with time and information to feed my fascination (actually obsession) with your dad and grandfather's work.

The very patient Wally Barton and Carlos Edwards, whose walks were hijacked.

Julie Power, the wonderful wordsmith.

My house buddies – what a tremendous little club of like-minded folks we are. I value our lovely friendships in whatever form they take and really appreciate your humour, energy, enthusiasm and guidance: Shannyn, Elle, Amanda, Nathan, Drew, Stu, Lord Fry Ash, Pam, Simon Pollack and Captain Sal.

My excellent walking partners, who see what I see and don't eyeroll when I say, 'How 'bout just one more street ... I've a got a feeling': Mel Barton, Jen and Nick the Knife-maker.

Jeanne Ryckmans, Kaz Willams and Benny Agius – everyone should have such wise women in their life.

Kate and Litza, who've been more helpful than they realise.

Simon Dance, you divine pedant.

The delightful Paul Kenny, for always being superbly Paul Kenny.

Tony Ng Kwok: Doh jeh.

Cosette Morris, my dear friend, for endless encouragement and bubbly sustenance.

Jane Hunterland, for being a legend.

My fabulous, supportive, lockdown-lifesaving Kiwi family Joan and Kevin.

All you nice people who wrote nice things about my pics to put in this book.

All the people who joined on the journey, taking the time to message me, telling me your own stories, sharing information, anecdotes, photos – you're great, thanks for coming along.

Vanessa Radnidge, for every bloody thing.

Everyone at Affirm Press, with extra love and thanks to Kelly, Liz, Ruby, Kevin, Emily, Rosie, Stephanie, Laura, Alistair, Keiran and Martin, and the awesome account managers.

Luke Causby, I've long been a fan. Thanks for my super cover, I love it.

Lastly, but not leastly, thanks to Hildegaard, the best partner for every single thing. I don't have enough words. You are the best. Chuck out the rest.

Sandy Weir started working in the Australian book trade in 1988 after a few years in retail following a disastrous HSC result. Sandy technically lives in country New South Wales but is most often found anywhere but there, looking over fences. She started sharing residential treasures on her Instagram page @other_peopleshomes in February 2022.

49